BEEN SPOKEN TO

BEEN SPOKEN TO

Matthew R Thomas

To order additional copies of this book, contact:
Xlibris
AU TFN: 1 800 844 927 (Toll Free inside Australia)
AU Local: (02) 8310 8187 (+61 2 8310 8187 from outside Australia)
www.Xlibris.com.au
Orders@Xlibris.com.au
858658

CONTENTS

ILLUSTRATIONS

- **PAGE 42** – HOME, A PAINTING CREATED BY MATTHEW RICHARD THOMAS. FEATURED WITHIN THE THANK YOU PAGE, TELLS THE STORY OF BEING PROUD OF YOUR HOME, AN INSPIRATION TAKEN FROM THE SUNSETS OF BROOM, WESTERN AUSTRALIA.

IN

LOVING

MEMORY

ERIC CHARLES THOMAS

AND

HILDA HARRISON

DEDICATION

This is dedicated to these amazing mothers.

Betty Thomas

Margaret Worn Harrison

Hilda Harrison

Leisa Thomas

Crystal Thomas

Val Robson

These people have contributed and have had a huge impact on myself and the community. The dedication and sacrifice shall be remembered for ever.

RESPECT

I respect the First Nations People past, present, and future.

Please be aware that there are images of people who
have now passed, and I acknowledge to respect the
use of these images for means of education.

I am a

Gunai/Kurnai man

my clan

Krauatungalung

my tribe

Kurnai

BEEN SPOKEN TO

CREATED IN 2023

The inspiration derived from my experiences in the Australian community. I have been raised in a non-indigenous world and later came to know where I came from and who I would have been. I found that I belong to two worlds. I am continuing to adjust while slowly learning my First Nations Culture. It is a challenge that is not impossible, but the challenges come in many forms as I try to negotiate my Biological Ancestral history with a non-indigenous Australian life.

I have much to learn of my culture and eager to pass on as much as I am allowed, to my family, and to the general community.

This light read will seem a little unorthodox.

It is raw and a little controversial.

It is the truth.

Some of my views you may disagree with and some you are going to like. I must keep in mind to preserve the moment of when I have written these pieces within this book. Some of what you read has been submitted to Australian Parliamentary figures with little response. It is at a time of cultural and community unrest of Australia's timeline. The time of Referendum, year 2023.

My true feelings are, there must be balance first. Therefore, dialog must be clear. Understanding language established. Education established.

I truly believe the founders of each clan of each tribe in Australia, would have wanted.

Balance first.

Quoted: The Hon Daniel Andrews MP

Premier of Victoria.

Dear Matthew Thomas

Along with the Victorian Government, we acknowledge the immense pain, suffering and despair placed upon you due to past government policies and laws.

We deeply and genuinely acknowledge your continued resilience, strength, and courage in your journey of recovery.

On behalf of the Victorian Government, we write to make this overdue apology to you.

The Victorian Government apologises for the forced removal from your family –

From your Country, community, culture, and language –

And for depriving you of your birthright by actions perpetrated on you.

We apologise for the extreme inhumane acts committed against you – the torture, the unspeakable hurt, and the intergenerational trauma that you and your family continue to carry and experience due to your removal.

We are sorry.

Together with the Victorian Government, we have reflected deeply on the inhumane acts and mistreatment of the Victorian Aboriginal Stolen Generations and acknowledge the role that the Victorian Government has played.

It is now the responsibility of the Victorian Government to ensure all Victorians are aware of the true history of Australia. That they are aware of the truth of what Stolen Generations like you have endured, and the everlasting impacts it causes for you, your family, and your future generations.

Our government will continue to be committed to building a positive future for all Aboriginal and Torres Strait islander peoples by improving their lives through self-determination.

Because without it, we can't move forward, and we can't improve First People's health, wellbeing, and human rights.

The Victorian Government respectfully intends that you receive this sincere apology in the spirit in which it is made and hope it helps you in some small way as part of your healing.

Yours sincerely

The Hon Daniel Andrews MP
Premier of Victoria

MY DREAMING

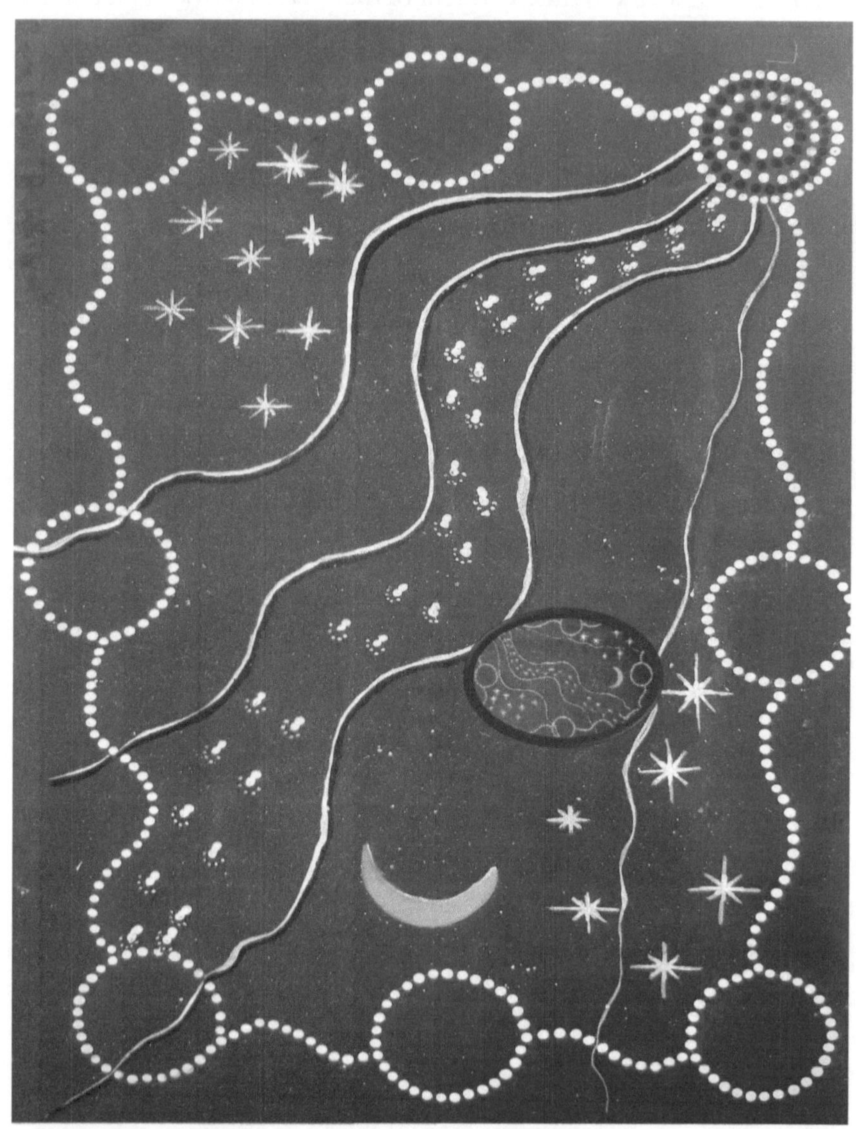

Painted by Margaret Worn Harrison.

BEEN SPOKEN TO

The tall trees are our ancestors' arms.
The treetops are their hands.
The roots are their feet.
The ocean is their stomach.
The sky is their mind.
The wind is their breath.
The sun is their father.
The earth is their mother.
The moon is their sister.

Written by
Matthew Richard Thomas
(Cedric Edward Harrison)
Proud Gunai/Kurnai man.

DREAMTIME

Painted by
Matthew Richard Thomas

THREE TRIBAL NATIONS

The two tribes will meet in a very public place with significant meaning socially and cohesive of all parties and collaboration of all governments to bear witness for all nations.

The building will cater for delegates from a far, as well as people from all walks. The governors of the state must be present as a mark of respect, and an opportunity for the two tribes to share a powerful cultural event.

The floor must be rectangle with delegates and guest on the outside to be the witness. The two tribes with their respective clans will have a side of the rectangle each. In this case one the West side and one on the East side. A distinctive line will separate the two. A large scale of cultural sand markings at the centre, mostly of those of the host tribe.

The two tribes will do their ceremonies in their own way for the other tribe to bear witness. Members of each respected clans approach the centre to pass on their message sticks. They then acknowledge that the two tribes will be diplomatically connected with spiritual and cultural ties. The birth of modern-day tribal Ambassadors.

An opportunity for the witness to share this day of significance. To mark this day to remember and to understand a common strive for all unity and peace.

Written by
Matthew Richard Thomas
(Cedric Edward Harrison)
Proud Gunai/Kurnai man

HARMONY

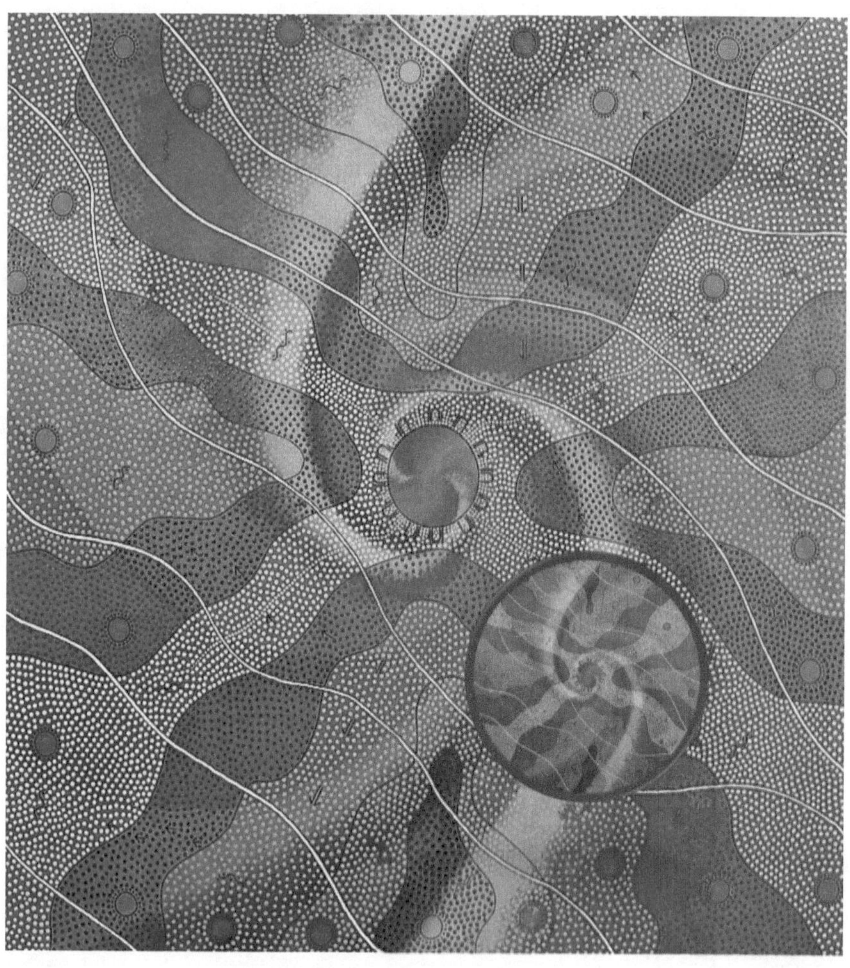

Painted by Matthew Richard Thomas

Hon Dr Tony Buti MLA

Minister for Education; Aboriginal Affairs;

Citizenship and Multicultural Interests

Our Ref: 80-07246

Mr Matthew Thomas Via email: xxxxxx(@)yahoo.com.au

Dear Mr Thomas

INDIGENOUS AUSTRALIA EMBASSY NETWORK PROPOSAL

Thank you for your correspondence dated 21 December 2022 to the Premier the Hon Mark McGowan MLA, who has asked me to respond on his behalf. I note that you previously written to me in relation to your proposal, and I sent you a response on 23 December 2022 which may have overlapped with your latest correspondence to the Premier. In my response, I had noted a range of possible funding sources within the Western Australian Government that may assist, and I encourage you to consider those options.

I would also like to thank you for providing details of your personal history and acknowledge the difficulties you and other members of the Stolen Generation have had to contend with.

Noting the details of your proposal, there may be potential links with the discussions underway about an Aboriginal and Torres Strait Islander Voice to the Australian Parliament. The Australian Government is currently preparing for a referendum on a constitutional amendment to allow for Aboriginal and Torres Strait Islander representation to

Parliament. Should the referendum be successful the Australian Government would likely need to develop processes Australia-wide to accommodate this change.

You can find out more information about the Voice process and timing at the following link: www.voice.niaa.gov.au/about Thank you again for taking the time to write to the WA Government and I wish you well in developing and pursuing your proposal.

Yours sincerely Dr Tony Buti MLA

MINISTER FOR ABORIGINAL AFFAIRS 1 I JAN 2023

THE PLACE OF MY

Spirit Resting

BUNGYUNDA

INDIGENOUS AUSTRALIAN EMBASSY NETWORK PROPOSAL

To embrace engagement with an ancient culture to find
out who you really are and enjoy the recognition with
country harmonizing and learning with others.

Created and written by
Matthew Richard Thomas
(Cedric Edward Harrison)
Proud Gunai/Kurnai man

INDIGENOUS AUSTRALIA EMBASSY NETWORK

- **Purpose:**

A semi profit organization with the ability to run efficiently and co-efficiently with collaborated organizations registered. To supply faster service for people who have just found out of their Aboriginal ties and do not know who to turn to. Lost Aboriginals who need help with connecting and gaining proof of Aboriginally. To connecting with their country through a clan member belonging to their country that can help guide them through a new experience from when raised in a non-indigenous environment. That our guides will have the understanding and will only work at a pace that each client is comfortable with until they have the strength to continue with confidence. To help with non-Indigenous partners/family and provide them with basic cultural awareness of the client's cultural origin. To help adoptive families with introducing cultural awareness and the biological family aid to provide them with understanding of pre and post cultural environments of the client. The Indigenous Embassy Network will could run from a hub at each major city under the care and nurture of the main local Indigenous group at each hub. Each hub can access a member of every country/clan group to aid. Each hub is an embassy for each Indigenous Australian Country. It is a vital link to other services within the network that they can easily access and referred for counselling and other health management organizations within the network.

Written by Matthew Richard Thomas – Proud GURAI KURNAI man 24/11/2022.

INDIGENOUS AUSTRALIA EMBASSY NETWORK

- **Infrastructure:**

The way this will supply is for a recognized elder or member of a particular group to become an ambassador. At each hub network will be an ambassador or representative that should supply a service within embassy standards. The network will be acting as one across the entire country in each major city. This will allow fast action across vast distances with quicker response times that can ease the closure process for the client. With the help of organizations collaborating with each state government, communications could be possible with mine site style communications to remote locations which will supply Aboriginal backed employment to set up and support. Coordination with the correct cultural handling of sensitive equipment supplied by Aboriginal back logistic companies is another employment opportunity. Each client that has obtained their cultural identity will automatically go into a data-based system that can be easily accessible, when needed without hindrance. This would access all Indigenous Australian Embassy Network hubs. Each hub will be able to cater for all the employers/volunteers with provided and up to date training and ongoing training to cope with diverse and challenging society.

Written by Matthew Richard Thomas – Proud GUNAI KURNAI man 24/11/2022.

INDIGENOUS AUSTRALIA EMBASSY NETWORK

- **Ideas**
- As part of this presentation to incorporate Indigenous groups around Australia to send in a video of what this means to them and pick 5 or 6 that stand out.
- To promote with design and networking planning.
- Talk to groups face to face or video link up.
- A plan to approach potential investors.
- Create a visual plan view of what the network will look like across Australia.
- Create an Embassy Network Matrix to enable a visual on performance and progress by enabling to show very quickly red flags and rectify it on a priority basis.
- Organize through the right channels for government intervention and commitment with planning ministers involved.
- Register the network name and make it official and patenting on the idea.

Written by Matthew Richard Thomas – Proud GUNAI KURNAI man 24/11/2022.

INDIGENOUS AUSTRALIA EMBASSY NETWORK

- **Infrastructure Cont.**

As part of the core of this program will try to create a safe haven for abused women from domestic violence within the Aboriginal community and will supply the immediate help and a way out from a hazardous environment as a priority and into the facility where they will be safe as well as effected children. The facility will be between 4 to 5 floors, each holding a central counseling hub and support network. It can also help with reuniting with family that can help ease their situation if they are interstate through the IAEN program. On each floor an array of self-contained rooms to cater for women on their own or in need with children dependent of their mother. The counselling will provide each effected individual with the tools to recovery and strengthen the ability for them to make decisions for themselves for a better future. A security network for each client is imperative and will be completely confidential so they can start their healing with the comfort of knowing that they will be safe.

Written by Matthew Richard Thomas – Proud GUNAI KURNAI man 06/12/2022.

COMMENTS

Around this time, I was going through a very deep depression as it was exceedingly difficult to prove that I was a First Nation person. The process took around seven months. However, I did take notice of the difficulties and put forward a proposal. Anything like a suggestion was a good start and it really was the first engagement I have had with a government. What led me to this was determination to improve on a current situation, which is all.

Soon the situation became more intense as I have heard about a voice to parliament from the First Nations people. My gut instinct was telling me something was not right, there is great unrest with this, but I could not pinpoint it.

As a First Nations person, I automatically felt a responsibility to act for the future of my ancestral teachings. I was worried and realized it felt deeply wrong in my heart. I have experienced things that may be difficult to understand, so I try to learn from them or decipher what they mean. I had to write a piece about annexation and the logical truth behind it. I had to compliment the next piece of writing that I would send to the government to help explain. This writing comes from my heart as I felt I would be writing for my ancestor's history, and the future of First Nations people with general Australia.

I was concerned and had to consult my adoptive brother for what he had to say on these concerning issues. What he wrote, I felt, was fair for all. I must always consider where I have come from and where my bloodlines run for thousands of years when considering the present population's needs.

I am doing my bit to slow down the process for fair gain.

Education first, understanding true history first, Understanding language first.

WALKABOUT

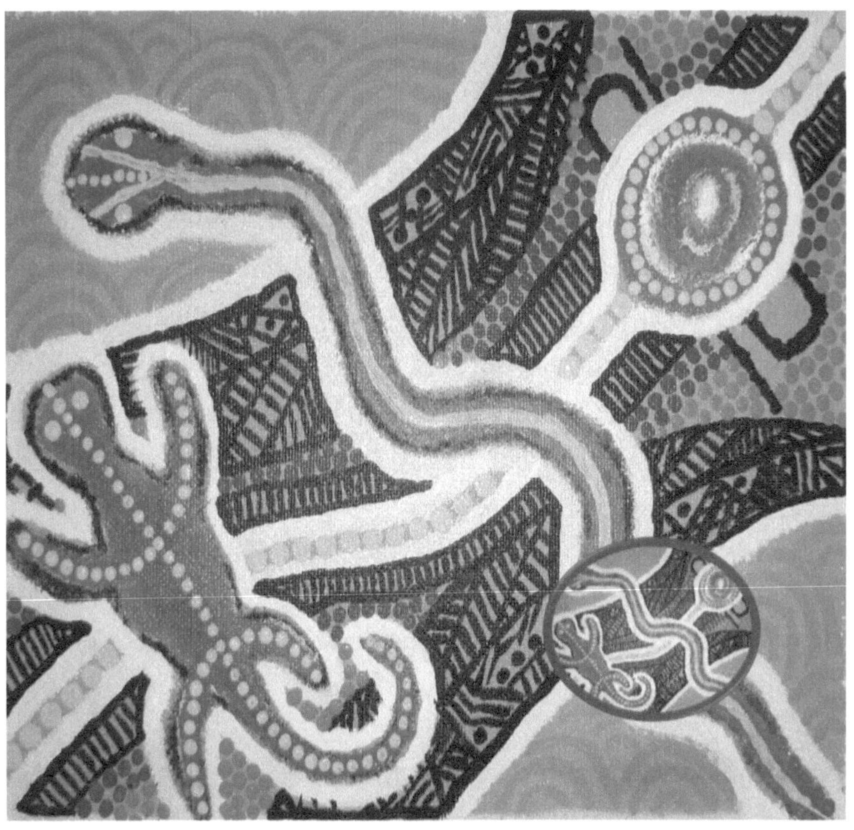

Painted by
Matthew Richard Thomas

A LETTER TO ME FROM MY BROTHER

Hi Matt,

Thanks for sending through, you have obviously thought about this a great deal, and I hope it gets traction.

I personally do not support a means whereby different people have different rights or privileges under the constitution. The constitution is the basis for all law and therefore we would not be equal under the law. In this there could be a united Australia. In essence this is what "The Voice" paves the way for and why it needs a referendum. The constitution can only be amended by referendum. As a point of interest, in 1967 the Australian people voted to give Aboriginal people the same rights under the constitution. Now the government is proposing a change to give unequal rights under the constitution.

However, do I agree that the following should be implemented or increased? Absolutely.

- Mandatory Aboriginal Cultural and history studies in school for all Australians.
- All workplaces over 50 employers to run mandatory cultural awareness and history training run by a local Aboriginal Cultural Leader i.e., we had this run by Lindsay Black form Blackworks, was an eye opener. Particularly multi-generational abuse.

- Access to specialist Aboriginal health care for remedial and preventative care in urban and remote areas.
- Structuring of education and learning for Aboriginal children and audits to provide structure and purpose.
- Rather than increased welfare, change to increase in tax concessions so that the more paid work undertaken, the better off Aboriginal people will be. Once people have active employment, this has massive benefits in having a purpose for life. Once someone has no purpose, their mental and physical health dramatically diminishes.
- Harsher penalties for racism and discrimination.

Just my 2 cents
Kind Regards
Rohan Charles Thomas

ANNEXATION

THE ANNEXATION OF PARTS OF UKRANE LEAD BY RUSSIA HAS CAUGHT THE ATTENTION OF WORLD LEADERS.

IT HAS HIGHTENED THE MEMERY OF THE UNRESOLVED ANNEXATION OF CRIMEA, ANOTHER PART OF UKRANE.

WHEN THE WORLD WITTNESSED RUSSIA ATTEMPTING TO HOLD A REFERENDUM INSIDE THE ANNEXED PART OF UKRANE, WORLD LEADERS CONDEMED THE ACTION.

SURELY THIS WOULD BE AN ACTION RECOGNISED AS ILLEGAL.

THEREFORE, SURELY A REFERENDUM WOULD NOT, AND WILL NOT, BE FORMALLY RECOGNISED, WITH ANY OUTCOME OF SUCH A REFERENDUM INSIDE A LEGAL STRUCTURE IF ANY ANNEXATION IS UNRESOLVED.

EVEN WITH THE GREATEST INTENSIONS FOR A NATION, CAN NOT BE DECIDED FOR A NATION, WHILE WITHIN ANNEXATION, NOT BEING RESOLVED BY THE HOST NATION/COUNTRY, AND THE EMPOSING NATION, BY AN AGREEMENT ON WHICH BOTH, SOLOMNY AGREE, OF A NOTION FORWARD, TO SAFELY SECURE, THE INTEGRITY OF ALL CITISENS, OF THE HOST NATION, IS FULLY RESTORED.

THEN, AND ONLY THEN, CAN A NATION REALEASED, FROM THE ANNEXATION, HAVE THE POWER, AND THAT POWER, CAN ONLY THEN BE RECOGNISED, UNDER THEIR OWN PROPOSED NOTIONS FOR THE WORLD TO BEAR WITNESS.

Written by
MATTHEW RICHARD THOMAS
(CEDRIC EDWARD HARRISON)
2023

PATH OF KNOWLERDGE

Painted by

Matthew Richard Thomas

ADDRESS TO THE COMMONWEALTH

Year 2023
TO HIS MAGESTY, THE KING,
TO THE PRIMINISTER, OF AUSTRALIA,
TO THE GOVERNOR,
TO ALL REPRESENTATIVES,
TO ALL WITNESSESS.

AS I, AS WE ALL, WILL FOREVER
RESPECT THE COUNTRY, WE NOW WALK ON
KNOWING WHAT IT WAS
AND
KNOWING WHAT IT WILL
WHILE REMAINING WHAT IT WAS

THE FOUNDER OF MY NATION TRIBE,
HIS NAME IS BORUN,
MY TRIBE IS KURNAI,
I AM A GUNAI/KURNAI MAN,
EIGHTEEN THOUSAND YEARS LATER,
I HAVE HIS BLOOD IN MY VIENS,
HE IS STILL AN INSPIRATION,

WE MUST TEACH YOU,
I WANT TO SHOW YOU,
I WANT TO TEACH YOU,

I WANT YOU TO EMBRACE

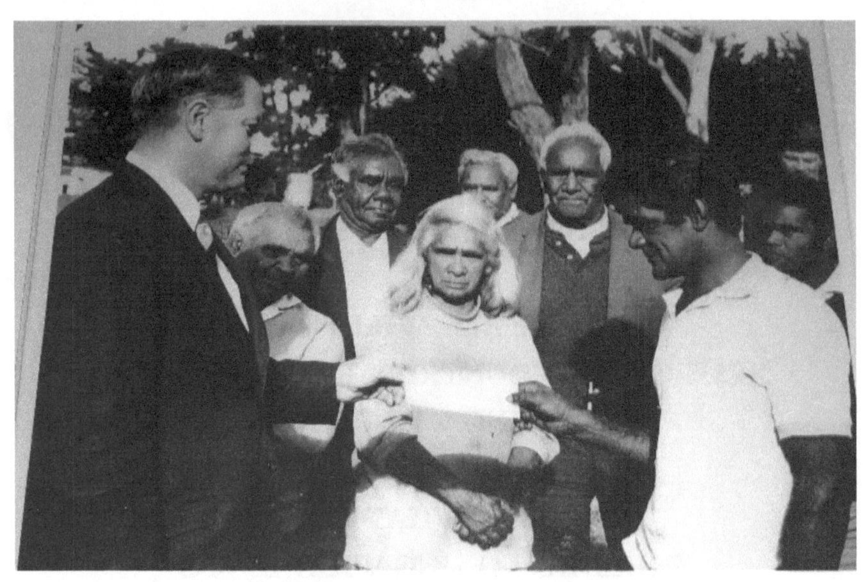

ACKNOWLEDGEMENT

FOR OVER SIXTY THOUSAND YEARS
THE TEACHINGS CAN CONTINUE.

TO THE ANCESTORS OF ALL OF THE FIRST NATIONS
OF THIS BEAUTIFUL COUNTRY, AUSTRALIA,
TO THOSE RESPONSIBLE FOR PASSING THE
KNOWLEDGE AND KEEPING TRADITIONS ALIVE,
TO THOSE WHO FOUGHT,
TO ALL SURVIVERS,
TO ALL THE BEAUTIFUL PEOPLE
PAST, PRESENT AND FUTURE
THAT STILL MAKE UP THE NATIONS THE
WORLD KNOWS AS AUSTRALIA.
WE OF A DIVERSE SOCIOTY APROACHING A NEW,

WILLINGLY AND FORMILY,

ACKNOWLEDGE

SPEECH

MY NAME IS MATTHEW RICHARD THOMAS, ALSO FORMALLY KNOWN AS CEDRIC EDWARD HARRISON.

YOU SEE THAT IS KIND OF NORMAL, HEARING THAT PEOPLE HAVE NAME CHANGES FOR REASONS.

IN MY CASE IT WAS ADOPTION, JUST A NORMAL FORMALITY WITH LOTS OF FORMS TO FILL OUT FOR THE PARENTS, NO DOUBT.

THIS WAS DIFFERENT, IT WAS AN ADOPTION AS A RESULT OF A STOLEN GENERATION INCIDENT. YES, MY FRIENDS, I AM PART OF THE STOLEN GENERATION. I WON'T GO INTO ALL THE DETAILS BECAUSE IT IS NOT A PLEASANT STORY, IT MAKES YOU FEEL UNCONFORTABLE, BUT WHEN YOU SEE ME NOW, ONE MIGHT SAY, WELL THAT WAS BACK THEN, AND ITS ALL-GOOD NOW, LOOK HES DOING ALLRIGHT. LOOK AT US NOW, WE ARE A GREAT SOCIOTY THAT CAN TRADE TO WORLD STANDARDS AND BE A TOP TOURIST DESTINATIONS WITH OUR VERY FRIENDLY CULTURE. YES, THIS IS TRUE, I LOVE THAT. WE HAVE BEEN GIVEN TOOLS OF LATE, TO HAVE A GOOD GO, AND I ENCOURAGE THAT.

AS THER ARE EXAMPLES OF SUCCESS OF THE FIRST NATIONS PEOPLE.

MY FRIENDS, AT WHAT COST?

WE MUST ASK OUR SELVES IN HOW DO WE EVALUATED A HUMAN LIFE, AND TIMES THAT BY ONE HUNDRED, AND TIMES THAT BY ONE HUNDRED MILLION.

IT MAKES NO DIFFERENCE. ONE HUMAN LIFE, TO ONE HUNDRED MILLION, IT HAS THE SAME EFFECTIVE RESPONSE OF WHO WAS BEFORE THEM.

WE ALL KNOW WHY THIS HAS TO BE ADDRESSED, BUT IM NOT ABOUT POINTING THE FINGER. IM ABOUT ASSURITTY THAT WE ALL LEARN TO WORK AS ONE.

TO COME TO RESOLUTION, IT IS EASY TO LOOK INTO YOUR HEART, BY LOOKING THROUGH THE EYES OF OTHERS. THIS ENSURES ONE CAN TRUST AND RESPECT.

BEFORE I GO ON, I WOULD LIKE TO EXPRESS AN EXPECTATION, WITH ALL DUE RESPECT. IT IS A BEAUTIFUL AND POWERFULL SNIPPIT FROM THE PAST. A PIECE BY THE GREAT MR HENRY FORD AND I THINK WE CAN ALL TAKE THIS ONBOARD.

UNITING TOGETHER IS A BEGINNING

KEEPING TOGETHER IS PROGRESS

WORKING TOGETHER IS SUCCESS

YOU KNOW, THAT TO ME IS TEAMWORK.

AS MR PRIMINISTER YOU MAY BEAR THE WEIGHT OF THIS FINE NATION. IN DOING THIS MR PRIMINISTER, I BEAR THE WEIGHT OF NATIONS.

MR PRIMINISTER, YOU AS A PERSON ARE A GREAT LEADER. TO BE PREPARED TO FOLLOW A DREAM, TO LEAD BY EXAMPLE. THAT IS EXACTLY WHY WE JOIN A PARTY, TO PATHE THE WAY. TO PATHE THE WAY NOT FOR ONESELF OR PERSONAL GAIN, BUT TO REALY STICK YOUR NECK OUT FOR A COURSE YOU TRULY BELIEVE IN. I CAN SEE THAT IN YOU. AS OTHER LEADERS. MR PRIMINISTER, YOUR HEART HAS SPOKEN TO YOU AND YOU CHOSE A PATH THAT CAN REALLY BE EFFECTIVE, A PATH THAT CAN BE THE START OF EMPOWERMENT TO NATIONS PROVIDED BY A VERY POTENTIALLY EFFECTIVE IDEA.

THAT IDEA, MR PRIMINISTER IS THE VOICE.

I CAN SEE AS WE ALL CAN, HOW PROWD YOU AND YOUR TEAM ARE. THE OPPERSITION SHOULD BE PRAISING YOU FOR YOUR KIND HEART. WITH ALL RESPECT, YOUR TEAM WILL LET YOU DOWN, AND HAS ALREADY LET YOU DOWN, AND UNFORTUNATLY THAT IS HOW IT LOOKS, BUT IT IS NOT ALL WASTED.

THIS HAS NOW GIVEN THE NATIONS OF AUSTRALIA THE PUSH THAT WE HAVE LONG NEEDED. IT HAS NOW BROUGHT THE ATTENTION TO THE WORLD, AND I PERSONALLY THANK YOU FOR THAT. IT HAS HIGHLIGHTED THE NEED, MR PRIMINISTER, THE

IMPORTANCE TO BEGIN THE PROCESS OF SIGNING A TWEATY BY THE HEAD OF THE STATE. A TRUE LEADER MUST RECOGNISE A NATION AND NATIONS WITHIN THAT NATION HAS THE ABILLITY TO RISE PEACEFULLY WITH THE CONTINUENCE OF THE CONSTITUTION AND BE PREPAIRED TO CONCIDER ALL OF THOSE THAT HAS GAINED SO MUCH FROM THE UNMENTIONABLE.

THE FACT.

I WILL TAKE YOU BACK TO WHAT I SAID. I SAID THAT I WILL NOT PIONT THE FINGER. NOR WILL I HAVE ANY HARD FEELINGS FOR TODAYS PEOPLES CULTURE. MY FRIENDS, I WILL NOT DENY YOU THE TRUTH ABOUT WHAT HAS HAPPENED TO THE NATIONS EITHER. WE ALL SEE, AND WE ALL MUST FEEL WHAT WE SEE TODAY. AN EXAMMPLE WE SEE TODAY. THERE IS A NATION THAT REMINDS ME OF AUSTRALIA, THEYRE FUNNY, THEYRE SMART AND EASY GOING.

I LOVE PEACE, AS SHOULD WE ALL. I LOVE A PEACEFULL, DEMOCRADIC, AND HARD WORKING SOCIOTY. I WORRY ABOUT THIS NATION AND WHAT I SEE IS ANOTHER, WANTING TO GAIN, BUT TO GAIN, BY ANNEXATION.

WE ALL KNOW WHAT WE SEE.

YES, WITHOUT ACKNOWLEDGEMENT, A LEADER CAN NOT MOVE FORWARD, ESPECIALLY WITH A WIEGHT OF NATIONS. ACKNOWLEDGEMENT IS NEEDED. AFTER

ACKNOWLEDGEMENT COMES LISTERNING AND THEN NEGOTIATING. WITHOUT HYSTORY,

A LEADER CAN NOT MAKE DESISSIONS, BECAUSE LEADERS RELY ON HYSTORY IN ORDER TO MAKE THE RIGHT DECISIONS.

A LEADER WILL ONLY BE WORTH, WHO THEY ARE LEADING.

I SAY THIS WITH A WEIGHT OF NATIONS OF AUSTRALIA.

NATIONS WHO HAVE HAD AND STILL CONTINUING TO DO SO, HAVE HAD DIPLOMITIC TIES WITH EACH OTHER FOR OVER SIXTY THOUSAND YEARS. THIS IS KNOWN. IT WOULD BE DIFFICULT TO DENY ANY ORGANISATION OF NATIONS WITH EXPERIENCE IN GOVERNING. IT SOUNDS KINDA UNREAL, DOSENT IT.

THE VOICE, MR PRIMINISTER, IS ONLY A METAPHORE. IT IS A GREAT IDEA, BUT WITHOUT POWER.

TO UNIFY AND BE EFFECTIVE. HAVE A TREATY SIGNED, ALLOW THE CONTINUENCE OF CULTURAL TEACHINGS – START BY TEACHING ABORIGINAL CULTURE AND LANGUAGE AS A BASIS FOR EVERY AUSTRALIAN. ALLOW FOR OVER SIXTY THOUSAND YEARS OF GOVERNING EXPERIENCE TO BE EMBRACED INTO TWO HUNDRED ODD YEARS OF COMMONWEALTH.

A SLOW AND PEACEFULL TRANSITION OF TWO DECADES SHOULD ENSURE UNDERSTANDING OF THE TRANSITION.

BY THEN, A GOVERNING LEGACY OF ONE EMPIRE HAS NOT BEEN DIMIINESHED BUT HAS SURVIVED WITH CHANGES THAT COINCIDE WITH AUSTRALIAS NATIONS.

WRITTEN BY
MATTHEW RICHARD THOMAS
(CEDRIC EDWARD HARRISON)
PROUD GUNAI/KURNAI MAN
IN HONOUR OF OUR FATHER
BORUN

ADDRESS TO PARLIAMENT

BY
MATTHEW RICHARD THOMAS
FORMALLY KNOWN AS
CEDRIC EDWARD HARRISON
A PROUD GUNAI/KURNAI MAN

As a person born of this land I am classed as an Australian, because the constitution says that. I have the same rights as everyone, I have the same opportunities as everyone. I have the same ability as everyone, to contribute to my family as well as contribute to my community. The same opportunity as everyone else to learn how to live, the knowledge to live and progress.

As a First Nations person I am born of this land and classed as an Australian, because the constitution says that. I have the same rights as everyone, I have the same opportunities as everyone. I have the same ability as everyone, to contribute to my family as well as contribute to my community. The same opportunity as everyone else to learn how to live, the knowledge to live and progress.

This is because, I am a Proud Gunai/Kurnai man ready to forgive but never forget, because I wish for progress.

Please, my brothers and sisters, consider this before the Voice Referendum

Written by Matthew Richard Thomas
Friday, 28th April 2023

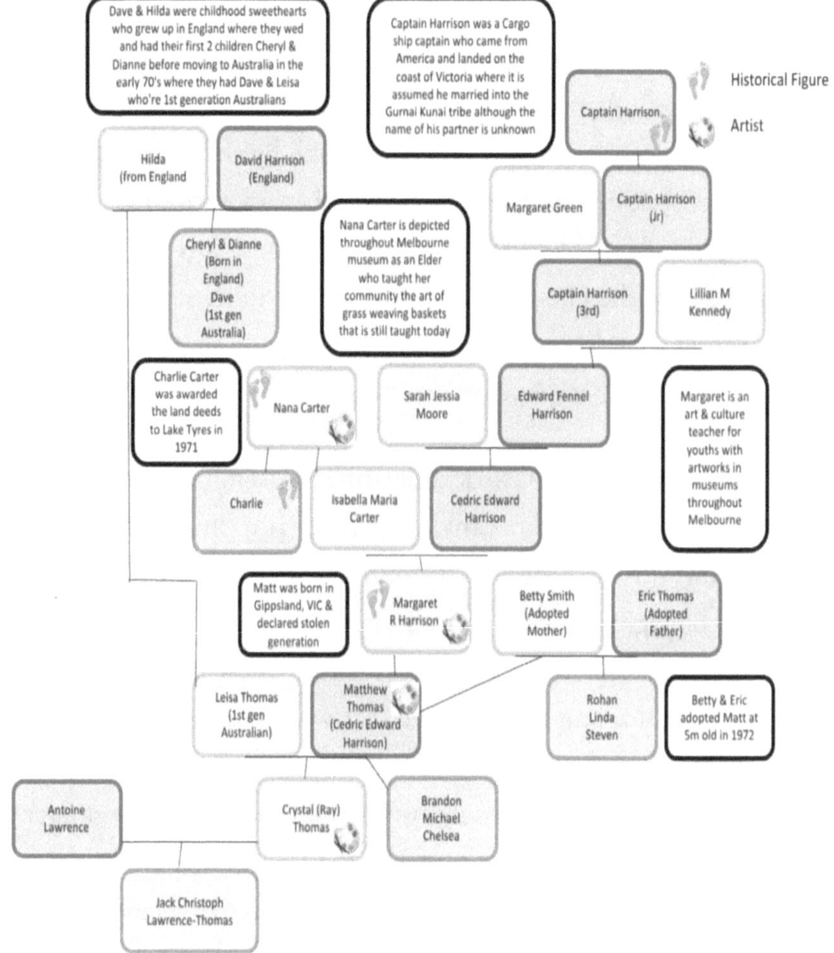
Dave & Hilda were childhood sweethearts who grew up in England where they wed and had their first 2 children Cheryl & Dianne before moving to Australia in the early 70's where they had Dave & Leisa who're 1st generation Australians

Captain Harrison was a Cargo ship captain who came from America and landed on the coast of Victoria where it is assumed he married into the Gurnai Kunai tribe although the name of his partner is unknown

Captain Harrison

Historical Figure

Artist

Hilda (from England

David Harrison (England)

Margaret Green

Captain Harrison (Jr)

Cheryl & Dianne (Born in England) Dave (1st gen Australia)

Nana Carter is depicted throughout Melbourne museum as an Elder who taught her community the art of grass weaving baskets that is still taught today

Captain Harrison (3rd)

Lillian M Kennedy

Charlie Carter was awarded the land deeds to Lake Tyres in 1971

Nana Carter

Sarah Jessia Moore

Edward Fennel Harrison

Margaret is an art & culture teacher for youths with artworks in museums throughout Melbourne

Charlie

Isabella Maria Carter

Cedric Edward Harrison

Matt was born in Gippsland, VIC & declared stolen generation

Margaret R Harrison

Betty Smith (Adopted Mother)

Eric Thomas (Adopted Father)

Leisa Thomas (1st gen Australian)

Matthew Thomas (Cedric Edward Harrison)

Rohan Linda Steven

Betty & Eric adopted Matt at 5m old in 1972

Antoine Lawrence

Crystal (Ray) Thomas

Brandon Michael Chelsea

Jack Christoph Lawrence-Thomas

I AM, OR AM I

Intro:

My name is Matthew Richard Thomas, and I was born, 1972 in Warragul, situated in Southeast Gippsland, Victoria, Australia and raised in Perth, Western Australia. According to written personal accounts, I was taken from my biological mother at birth by the government and placed under state care for 5 months. I was then adopted to a truly kind and loving family. A blessing for one family and a loss for another as I had no idea of the circumstances that led up to these extraordinary events, and of what kind of effects it would have in time to come, well not for at least another 30 years later.

My name at birth was "Cedric Edward Harrison," named after my biological grandfather who came from a lengthy line of Indigenous family history in the area and surrounding areas of the place of my birth. My biological family had all experienced life on the missions which was very tough, because on the missions' Indigenous people were forced from a traditional life to a life that was more fitting for society. Other Indigenous people pulled through and were able to live within the system, others have been successful, and others were not so lucky, struggling with change in structure. I would say most are carrying scars with them and have not been at peace since, taken that a race of people that have had their laws, values, and diplomatic boundaries in place for around 50,000 years before recorded colonization began.

My biological family has history at Lake Tyers mission in Victoria, Australia. The tribe that I was born from is called the Kurnai Tribe. A very spiritual tribe that has an extraordinarily strong spiritual connection with the land. My biological mother who was searching for me since my birth found me after thirty years and we finally met at Perth Airport, Australia with the magazine company "Take Five" were taking photos. The meeting was very emotional with my wife and kids present to share the moment, which made the experience so happy and memorable.

It was a perfect situation being able to finally meet and share each other's life experiences and to be taught about some of the cultures that I have missed. After travelling to Victoria, Australia and meeting my biological family is when it started to go downhill for me, and the reality set in. I began to suffer with depression, anxiety, and a sense of not belonging to any society, not being able to fit in properly, remembering how I have been treated by society growing up, not understanding why. I could not stay in touch with my biological family and could not explain why. A roller-coaster ride with emotions going up and down. The feeling of being pulled apart from all sides. It was happening too fast with what seemed like dramatic changes were happening and even though I was 30 years old at the time, I felt like I was a lost boy with nowhere to go.

The struggle for me now, after 20 years is still real, the same struggle is real for my family, A struggle that will continue, but will become easier over time as new learning and development for Australia's First Nations people within our curriculum becomes a reality for all to learn and understand.

Cedric Edward Harrison
Known as
Matthew Richard Thomas
2022

MY STORY

The words entered my mind when my wife and I were discussing how to compile this life story together, realizing that there is more to this than we expected, I mean a whole lot more, and those words were strong and meaningful. The sheer scale of where it all began, right up to where we are now. I am talking about the name. The name "Harrison" which as mentioned earlier was the name of my birth. My name at birth was "Cedric Edward Harrison" before it changed five months after my birth. Remarkably interesting because my wife's family name was also "Harrison. As I was growing up in a non- Indigenous society within Australia, my name was changed when adopted out to become "Matthew Richard Thomas", and while growing up I had no idea at all that my previous name at birth had the name of "Harrison", I later found out at the age of thirty.

So where does that leave me and my beautiful wife in all of this? You see, my wife and I may have stumbled on something that may have connected both her family and my biological family in the past. The past around the time of colonization of Victoria, Australia. Apparently

- **DOT POINT Timeline**
- 1863 is the earliest date of the family tree.
- Suspect Names: John Harrison – James Harrison – William Harrison –
- So far, we suspect that John Harrison is from England close to Dave Harrison's family are from.

- We suspect a family member with the name "Harrison" (Capt. Harrison) interacted with local indigenous people between 1830/1860 -
- Moving forward – Margaret's Mum n Dad – A bit of background –
- The Carters – A bit of background – Great Uncle Charlie Carter -
- Margaret – A bit of background - separations – What happened at my birth –
- Matty's accounts - Brief history of my self – A bit of background – Family -
- The meeting – Teachings – experiences – Art -
- The effects for years -
- Artwork – Sharing -
- Litigation process – Findings made public -
- Summary –
- Where was I held for 5 months before adoption took place?
- Margaret (Biological Mother) was tricked into signing.
- I was sexually molested by a good salvation army person.

MATTYS ACCOUNTS:

I can remember far back as around 3 years old when I ran away from home. I knew exactly where I was, I was just exploring while hiding behind a wall of one of our neighbor's houses looking at mum. I did that more than enough but could not explain why, I often wonder if it had anything to do with subconscious displacement as a result from being taken from a mother straight after birth. It would have been horrific for her, as she was told that we were just doing some hearing test on your son, and that is it, she got to hold me for only a minute, and I was gone from her life forever. I ask, would it ever be possible for a young child to suffer a form of displacement from birth subconsciously? I guess that can be open for study further down the track. While I was young, I remember I would naturally relate to the land growing up, always having a good relationship with all animals, and had gone walk about once or twice without notice. I was different to my siblings growing up because I had issues which I could not explain while growing up, but my family have always been and still are truly kind and accepting. They treated me as their own from the moment I was adopted at 5 months old. I was taken somewhere under government control from birth to 5 months old, but I have no idea on the location and conditions I was kept under. Mum and Dad who came and picked me up is who I still call Mum and Dad today. They raised me in Perth, Western Australia in a suburb called Thornlie with a brother and a sister. We were originally living in Melbourne, Victoria, Australia until I was 2 years old, then moved up to Gladstone, Queensland, Australia for a brief time and then to Perth, Western Australia.

- Margaret (Biological Mother) – According to accounts my biological mother, she was dragged out of Warragul Hospital screaming with her heels dragging on the ground after they took me away as a newborn baby from her by force. She was forced and tricked into signing the adoption form that enabled me to be released. Judging by the way she was screaming on that day and thirty years of searching for me relentlessly, I do not think a mother such as Margaret that has reacted in this way, could give me away on her own accord. No, I do not think so. This is part of a policy by the government to separate half and quarter cast children from their biological families, taken away from their country, taken away from their culture, taken away from their religion, to be adjusted for society and eventually bred out. Yes, I ask if this is too much to hear, to accept the truth, to be taught this type of history in our schools. I totally get it that it would be difficult to include all of this in our history at schools because I would imagine knowing that a distant relative or ancestor that would have been involved or fully aware or in support of such practices, it was a difficult change for everyone. It can be and is hard to swallow but unfortunately this is the truth, and it must be taught, not to demonize but to show the world that the first Australians with their culture is still intact and that we can all learn from this. For the future generations of a multicultural society to have a newfound respect for the land and the first people's culture to work together, to live in harmony, to learn, to listen, to take seriously and to act to encourage everybody to learn the first people's culture and language. I would imagine it would influence the way society behaves towards the land and each other and may mold future governments to act in accordance with indigenous laws and culture, influencing decision making when it comes to mining, leasing, land management which we are already starting to see and maybe approaching foreign affairs differently and diversly to suit not only the wider community of Australia, but also Australia's first people.

This is where I wish to stop,
until next time.

Book written by
Matthew Richard Thomas
(Cedric Edward Harrison)
Proud Gunai/Kurnai man
2023

GREATFULLNESS IS EARNT WHEN IT IS SHARED

Written By

Matthew Richard THOMAS

Artwork "HOME" painted by Matthew R Thomas

THANK YOU

www.ingramcontent.com/pod-product-compliance
Lightning Source LLC
Chambersburg PA
CBHW031429250726
48656CB00002B/901